sex
true or false?

But if in your fear
you would seek
only love's peace
and love's pleasure,
Then it is better for you
that you cover your nakedness
and pass out of love's threshing-floor,
Into the seasonless world
where you shall laugh,
but not all of your laughter,
and weep,
but not all of your tears.

— KAHLIL GIBRAN, *The Prophet*

SEX
True or False?
The Pleasures, Perils and Passion of Sexual Intimacy

Michelle Rios Rice Hennelly
and R. Kevin Hennelly

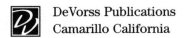

DeVorss Publications
Camarillo California

Sex: True or False?

Copyright © 2003
Michelle Rios Rice Hennelly and R. Kevin Hennelly
ISBN: 0-87516-784-5
Library of Congress Control Number: 2002106288

DeVorss & Company, *Publishers*
PO Box 1389
Camarillo, CA 93011-1389
USA

www.devorss.com

Printed in the United States of America

This book is dedicated to children of all ages in the hope that in their innocence they will always know the abundant grace, power, and beauty of sexual energy and that through this miraculous gift they will bring healing and transformation to themselves and the world. We give special thanks to those children in our life who continuously remind us of the love and joy we are meant to be.

contents

Love comforteth like sunshine after rain,
But lust's effect is tempest after sun;
Love's gentle spring doth always fresh remain,
Lust's winter comes ere summer half be done;
Love surfeits not, lust like a glutton dies;
Love is all truth, lust full of forgèd lies.

— SHAKESPEARE, *Venus & Adonis*

preface

Unlike a recent book that seeks to "create a public life that is erotic," *Sex: True or False?* aims at a personal life that is *profoundly sexual*. It proposes a more complete understanding of love-making and the energies related to it, as well as the place they rightly occupy in our lives.

In an era when sex is a no-holds-barred subject where "anything goes," how are we relating to it and what use are we making of our sexual energies? Have we an adequate view of their titanic power and the consequences of their misuse?

A popular song asks still another question: "What has *love* got to do with it?"

The answer is: *Everything.*

Sexual energies are misused when they are not used in relation to love.

There is no question that many, perhaps most, of us make some misuse of our body and sexual energies, having lost— or never having had—an understanding of them in their integrity and the role it is their nature to play in our lives. We shall consider these energies and what happens when they are used both wholesomely and unwholesomely.

When love-making is experienced at a low level of consciousness and is confused with mere sex, the results for mind and body can be exceedingly harmful. Some of the consequences include energy blockage and depletion; emotional numbness; susceptibility and fatigue; negative energy exchanges; sexual "vampirism" (in which energy is literally robbed); submergence and loss of identity; and mental/physical disease. All of these problems are widespread and much in evidence, and most people do not recognize that they are caused, in whole or in part, by the misuse of, and wrong relationship to, sexual energy.

Sex: True or False? examines the consequences of loveless sex and contrasts them with the expansion of self that can occur in true *love*-making. *Loving* sex "opens" us energetically, bringing a greater abundance and vibrancy of energy to our personalities and lives. We *feel* stronger and more alive, and our personalities enjoy a greater creative force and power. We are healthier physically, and our mental awareness is heightened. This is because love, and the energy of love, is being experienced at the highest *reciprocal* level—the true use of sex.

With the end of the Victorian era a century ago, it was widely hoped that sexual hypocrisy and the sham of loveless but "respectable" and indissoluble arrangements would yield to an enlightened age in which love and sex would be ideally mated. The plentiful evidence to the contrary that surrounds us on all sides is sad proof that this utopia has not been realized.

Instead, by the 1920s it had taken only a single generation to tout the circumvention of sexual integrity and responsibility in the name of "free love"—a euphemism for loveless sex. Some forty years later, a confused culture would consider itself sexually "emancipated," rid at last of moral "hang-ups." We have ever since been solemnly urged by cultural gurus, especially those in the media and the entertainment industry, to "just do it."

We *are* just doing "it," and not all of the consequences are very happy. We are increasingly troubled and lost, coping with the cumulative effects of the misuse of the body and sexual energy over the course of several generations—as our burdened medical, mental health, and other social institutions amply demonstrate.

The misuse of sexual energy today reaches what might be considered epidemic levels, and we are just beginning to recognize its ruinous effects on both individual and collective planes. As so often happens with mass culture and its paroxysms, a time of reckoning and reconsideration finally comes round, and accounts—individual and collective—have to be settled.

For the reasoning person, this should not prove too daunting or even unwelcome. We are, after all, beings perpetually in quest of happiness, and one of the benefits of our more information-oriented society is the growing awareness that we are also *complex* beings, who are not well served by willful ignorance, simple-mindedness, instant gratification, quick fixes, and "messing around" with our lives. We are becoming increasingly aware that we exist simultaneously on many subtle levels; and, almost invariably, some place within us, *we do know better.*

We often sense something amiss in our sexual lives. We often feel unfulfilled and restless in our sexual relations. But we seldom fathom what is wrong or what is missing. Turning to *more* sex or turning *away from* sex altogether does not solve the problem. The solution is found in understanding sexual energy and its purpose and place in our lives.

Sex: True or False? poses the not-too-disagreeable task of looking our lives straight in the eye and realizing that *love* is at once our deepest need and our profoundest resource. Therefore it must accompany us to, and be found at, *all* our points of contact, all our destinations, all our rendezvous. Certainly this holds supremely true of our sexual energies and our sexual "being in the world." Whether in motel bed or marriage bed, we can fake nothing and get away with it.

Sex: True or False? is a no-holds-barred approach to its no-holds-barred subject. It is meant to be challenging. More than that, it will prove helpful, healing, and a guide to *genuine* sexual emancipation (and not the cheap imitation of emancipation that we may have misguidedly pursued), because *you*—the *entirety* of you—are this book's premise and its goal.

PART ONE

The True Power of Love-Making

LOVE IS SOMETHING THAT ONE BECOMES. Transformed by the power of love, one *becomes* love. It is an experience of being—for some, the *supreme* experience. It is a becoming that takes us out of the "ordinary" mind and into the mind of the heart. But too few know it as this.

Instead, love, if experienced at all, is often encountered at a low level of consciousness. This is because most of us *live* at a low level of consciousness and have not yet come to know and experience the fullness of love. It may carry with it the experience of nothing more than the *minimal human*, with the many limitations that implies. But there is another way, which opens us to the depths of love and lifts us into a higher level of consciousness.

When two persons *genuinely fall in love,* they open to love at a higher level. As their hearts and minds open to each other, they move closer to the truth of a deeper love that lies within them. This experience is the essence of what has been called romantic love.

Romantic love is not at all a trite term, though it is much misunderstood. An experience intimately linked to true love-making, it has three defining characteristics:

1. First, it is an opening to a higher-than-ordinary energy that we carry within. This energy is of our very essence, and opening to it accounts for the sense of joy and ecstasy that often accompanies being genuinely in love. We suddenly feel most alive to who we really are.

2. The second defining characteristic of romantic love is a desire to merge with and become one with the beloved.

3. The third characteristic is a longing for something transcendent—the more than *minimally* human—which takes us out of our ordinary consciousness and into the consciousness of love.

Romantic love is not about "projection," as some insist. Rather, it is first and foremost about *opening up of one's self—one's "heart."* If this is not *open,* and you project the contents of your mind onto another person, mistaking that for love, you become involved in a tangle deriving from the mind's delusions. The "heart," in contrast, leads to the truth of oneself, not to delusions.

Romantic love is an experience that wells up from our deepest nature. It is in this deepest part of our being, from which romantic love first emerges, that the *energy* of this love begins to flourish with that "other" who is more to us than a body. We experience the love that is our essence; we

4

merge with the beloved; and we transcend the limitations of ordinary consciousness.

It is the nature of love-making to bring together both our sexual energy and the love energy. When this occurs, the spark of love kindled in the first stirring of romantic love grows and becomes a flame of love that can bring romantic love to its fullest expression.

It is the task of the lovers, then, to protect and nurture the spark that comes alive within them at this special time so that it is not extinguished but instead grows stronger and deeper. Yet it is precisely here that the experience of romantic love runs aground for many.

In part this is because love in general, and romantic love in particular, are waylaid and attacked at almost every turn in today's world. Popular culture frequently portrays love as lust, confusing these two in the minds of many, especially the impressionable young who are too easily misled about love and the body. Yet *the energies of love and sex are different,* and their relation to each other must be properly understood.

So the task of two lovers is not only to protect and nurture the spark of genuine love that has come alive within them, but to grasp what they *truly* aspire to in romantic relationship and in the role of love-making. This, in turn, requires an understanding of the *energies* of love-making and their power to move human love into something far greater. If this new understanding is allowed to shape their consciousness and experiences, they come to know themselves in a new way and comprehend, perhaps for the first time, what love-making can truly be.

Your body needs to be held and to hold, to be touched and to touch. None of these needs is to be despised, denied, or repressed. But you have to keep searching for your body's deeper need, the need for genuine love. Every time you are able to go beyond the body's superficial desires for love, you are bringing your body home and moving toward integration and unity.

— HENRI NOUWEN

1

the energies
of love-making

THE IMPORTANCE OF SUBTLE BUT NOTICEABLE ENERGIES and their effects on physical health, as well as on mental and emotional well-being, is increasingly making itself felt in contemporary Western society, although many "traditional" societies have long recognized the importance of these energies for individual and even social welfare.

Many of these societies have found such energies in nature and have frequently based their spiritual values on them at many levels, using them to heal body, mind, and spirit—and to rise to, and live at, a higher consciousness.

Energy affects us on all levels, and we are coming to see the necessity for building our lives and societies in no small part around this fact. This is especially true of human relationships, which involve energy, and exchanges of energy, on many levels.

Individually, we need to develop our innate ability to feel these energies and know how they affect our lives. The world becomes a different place when we do so. Decisions can be reliably based on this kind of knowing; people, places, and activities can be assessed for the benefit or harm they may bring us.

Love-making and sex have an enormous impact on subtle energies, and these in turn affect us on many levels, including the physical, emotional, and mental. To this some would add the spiritual. The experience of sexual intercourse, however commonplace, is very complex energetically, and it is loaded with potential for great benefit or great harm.

In this section, then, we examine these energies in their dynamic nature and context.

A FIELD OF ENERGY

Each of us is surrounded by a "field" of energy that permeates the physical body, providing us with the fuel to function physically, emotionally, and mentally. The field around a person consists of energies that are often referred to as subtle, or nonphysical, "bodies" surrounding and permeating the physical body. These subtle bodies contain energy centers that are vital to the amount and movement of energy in the field surrounding a person.

When these centers are "open" and their energies vibrant and flowing, our energy fields are stronger and more resonant. This, in turn, confers on our personalities a greater creative force and power, so that we feel healthier and more energetic on every level. People with an abundance of this life-force are often perceived as vital and even charismatic, precisely because of the power of this energy.

However, energy can be used for *positive* or *negative* purposes; and when the energy centers are blocked or damaged or otherwise depleted for whatever reason, our bodies and personalities undergo loss of power and creative force.

As a result, we do not feel truly alive and strong, nor do we function at maximal levels.

DEPLETION AND EXPANSION

When this energy is lacking, we feel it. For example, when our energy field is depleted, we often feel physically tired or mentally/emotionally drained. At such times our energy field actually diminishes in size. Similarly, if one or more of the energy centers is blocked, closed, or otherwise damaged, our energy field diminishes, with its potential decreased. The resulting lack or imbalance can cause physical disease or mental/emotional disorder. (Of course, there are apparent exceptions; an elderly person may be physically weak because of age but still possess a vibrant energy field.) In any case, we cannot live and function at a high level if we do not have the energy for it.

OUR ENERGY FIELD REFLECTS OUR CONSCIOUSNESS

For most of us, the energy field reflects the state of our consciousness on different levels—a "mirror" of what we are carrying, e.g. physically, emotionally, mentally. For example, physical illnesses often show themselves in our energy field before they manifest in the body. Our thoughts and emotions, which are forms of energy, are therefore also carried and reflected in the energy field.

Not surprisingly, positive thoughts and emotions are generally reflected in positive flows of energy, while nega-

11

tive thoughts and emotions are generally reflected in dim or dark shades and constricted or disturbed flows. *This is true even if we are unaware of our thoughts and emotions.* What we *believe* we are thinking or feeling on a conscious level is often belied by what is reflected in our energy field. This is because *the energy field and its different levels and centers are closely connected to the subconscious mind.* Thus, the awareness and release of negative emotions or experiences subconsciously held will be reflected in changes for the better in a person's energy field.

An understanding of the energies that compose our energy field allows us to understand the relation of the energy centers to love-making and also to grasp how love-making relates to expanded awareness. Without an understanding of these energies and their place in love-making, we are very likely to misuse them, with harmful consequences for ourselves and our partners.

PERSONAL AND GLOBAL TRANSFORMATION

We have already noted that these energies are also necessary for us to move into, and remain at, higher levels of consciousness. Many of the experiences we aspire to—including those that lie beyond the merely physical, and some associated with spiritual awareness—are dependent on the energies' abundance and vibrancy.

In fact, the energies that make up our energy field are so powerful that, through their proper use, we can both transform ourselves and begin to transform the world around us. When life-force energies are joined with the energy of love *and are held in a distinct consciousness of love,* there is little good that we cannot accomplish.

That is why it is so important to cultivate these energies, and one of the ways is to understand their use in love-making: because if we can understand the true nature and design of the body and sexual energies, and if we can use them in alignment with love, we shall be helping to heal the world of one of its principal sources of mental/emotional turbulence and imbalance.

IN HARM'S WAY

We harm ourselves when we misuse the body and these energies. *They are misused when they are not used in relation to love.* Improper use causes "dark," negative imprints and energy to accumulate in the energy centers and field. This causes the energy centers to be damaged and become blocked, resulting in impaired and weakened energy within the centers, impaired flow of energy throughout the energy field, and quite possibly a blockage of the energy itself, and even its depletion.

When the energy centers are damaged or the energy flow is blocked, we become weakened energetically. We lose our vitality and must then struggle—or may even find ourselves unable—to expand our weakened energy and consciousness. This is an important reason, as we shall see, why we must guard so forcefully against the misuse of our body and sexual energies.

It is also why we should begin to regard promotion of these misuses in the media and popular culture as a cancer in the body of society. We are continually exposed to this when, through television or film or in other ways, we open our minds and feelings to a culture in which the misuse of the body and sexuality is promoted and even glorified. Sowing seeds of lust while teaching people, especially the young, the misuse of the body and sexual energies poisons our understanding of love-making and leads to attitudes and behaviors that damage us energetically.

Once we understand what we do to ourselves when we misuse the body and sexual energies, we see that the problem is much greater than we have thought and that there is nothing innocent about what the media and entertainment industries are doing. Part of the problem, of course, is that—unlike some traditional societies—we have lost an understanding of these energies and therefore do not recognize the harm we are doing to ourselves and others when we misuse them—*or when we are "entertained" by seeing them misused.*

POSSIBILITY OF A DRAMATIC DIFFERENCE

Let it not be supposed that such misuse is limited to sex outside of marriage—the conventional concept. Rather, it happens whenever two people—*even people who are married*—engage in sexual activity without love and openness. But if they come to understand love-making and its energies as precious, even "sacred," they can effect a dramatic change in their relationship and lives.

For those consciously on a spiritual path, love-making and its energies can be approached as a means of connecting with their spiritual nature and rising to a higher level of consciousness. Understanding the energies of love-making can also heal the conflict some religious people feel between physical desire and their desire for oneness with God.

The energies we feel so strongly in the body should, when understood correctly and used properly, only promote, not hinder, desire for transcendence and union with something greater. Almost all spiritual traditions recognize that true union with "something greater" comes with the opening of the heart. Love-making is one of the ways we have to bring about that opening.

All positive approaches to love-making, whether or not they encompass a spiritual dimension, aim at a wholeness of being that eludes us unless we are aware of the magnitude of the forces we are dealing with. A discussion of this wholeness follows.

2

the wholeness of love-making

FEW OF US GRASP THE *WHOLENESS* that is love-making. In true love-making, two people come together, open in body, mind, heart, and soul. They are intimate in *love*, and they join together and become one. They move together with pleasure toward an ecstatic moment. It is a moment beyond words, thoughts, form, and separateness—a state of bliss. They come to experience their own, and perhaps a still greater, *wholeness*. A part of what occurs in this moment is that they experience a loss of their *ordinary,* "minimal" self, and in its place they experience a greater fullness.

When we experience this greater fullness of self, we *know* in a different way than we ordinarily do through *minimal* self, which knows only through the ordinary, commonplace, outer-oriented mind—a limited way of knowing that prevents us from experiencing ourselves as we truly are.

When we move beyond minimal self and ordinary mind, we let go of much of what we *think* we are and move into something immensely greater. We move beyond the delusions of the commonplace, day-to-day mind and connect with something that cannot quite be known by means of that mind, with its limited concepts, ideas, and perceptions. We move into the mind of love that sits deep within us.

ORGASM: MOMENT OF TRUTH

In love-making, and especially at the moment of orgasm, we experience the *wholeness* of love. Be it only for a moment, we experience something we can call our *true* mind, the mind of love. We step beyond words, thoughts, and concepts. We even move beyond time. And as we surrender to love, the seed of truth within us comes to life. We momentarily lose all self-centered sense, *including the physical,* and move into a *totality* of love. We experience bliss and freedom, and in this experience we catch a glimpse of who we truly are. Sadly, it is an experience that most of us fail to know or else fail to recognize for what it truly is.

While love-making and orgasm are among our most pleasurable physical experiences, their greater capacity is to take us beyond physical pleasure. We long for wholeness, union, love. We long for the healing of our deepest wounds, which come from our separation from love. Many people, if only within, are desperately searching and crying out for peace, for satisfaction, for truth, for love. In genuine love-making, we find at least a temporary satisfaction of these longings, one that may even be pointing us to a more permanent satisfaction and the wounds' deepest healing.

BUT ONLY FOR A MOMENT?

This satisfaction may be momentary only because we have not yet come to know and experience love in the fullness of its beauty and power—its *reality* (and ours). When we do, the experience will remain alive within us. We shall no longer *glimpse* the wholeness of love; we shall *become* it. Here, then, we find the true meaning of love-making and orgasm.

CREATIVE NATURE OF LOVE-MAKING AND ORGASM

It is important to understand the nature of love-making and orgasm. Being more than merely physical beings, during love-making we encounter levels of experience that go beyond the physical and emotional. Here we characterize them as *energetic;* they are also regarded by some as spiritual in nature.

Love-making and orgasm create an expansion of energy in the energy fields of the lovers when the sexual energy merges with the deeper, more profound energy of love. These two potent forces converge only if the lovers' hearts are open and the centers associated with sexual energy are open and their energies flowing. This powerful fusion fills the lovers and their energy fields with the creative, blissful, healing energy of love, reaching its climax in orgasm.

The lovers experience this energy flowing in them, around them, and between them. Such expansion of energy has the power to move them into a still higher *vibrancy* of energy and an even higher level of *awareness*. Further, in orgasm it is possible to experience something like *formlessness*—a moment in which we experience intensely, and know directly, what we can only conceive of as our very "essence."

What we experience in love's orgasm allows us to know that *we are love* and that *we too can create life*—and not just biological life—*out of love*. We can give birth to love and beget enlightenment on many levels and in many ways. We can begin to know ourselves as much more than physical beings and experience ourselves outside of our ordinary, mundane consciousness.

We can also know that, underneath our perceptions and concepts—and beyond the limitations of the body—we are getting at the "truth" of ourselves. In love's orgasm, however briefly, we experience the reality and truth of who (or what) we really are. We experience our purest and highest energy, which is love.

ORGASM: PORTAL OF THE EXTRAORDINARY

Because of the profound nature of love-making and orgasm, when we come together with another in love-making, we experience a sense of beauty and wonder. When we are open and the sexual energy joins with the vital energy of love, we step out of the ordinary into the extraordinary—a state of bliss, the potential for which we first began to feel in the initial stirrings of romantic love.

Something very true, very real, comes to life at that time. We feel within us, and in the relationship with the beloved, the dance, the bliss of pure love and want to remain forever in this state. We want to touch and feel this love just as we want to touch and feel the beloved and to be touched and felt by him/her. We want to make love and to create over and over again this experience of love.

The experience, however, does not happen in isolation apart from who and what we are in other parts of ourselves and other areas of our lives. Life is more than a bedroom. *What we experience in love-making and orgasm is a reflection of the degree of wholeness we have achieved and the integrity that exists in all areas of our lives.*

When we bring to love-making a *consciousness* of love and a *desire to be open and intimate* with another in love, then the fullness of love can come alive within us. In contrast, when we bring to love-making a desire for something other than love and a lack of openness to the other, our experience of love-making and orgasm will reflect this. In other words, for better or worse, *we bring to the experience who and what we are,* and this will determine what the experience is for us.

AND A PERFECT UNION

It is no wonder, then, that so many people are desperately searching for meaning and even transcendence in romantic relationships. Each time we truly make love, join together with another intimately and with an open heart, we are enjoying the experience of something authentically *us,* intimately true to *ourselves.* At the same time, in these experiences we have the opportunity to join *completely* with another. There is no separation; there are no boundaries, no "private" thoughts or self-consciousness. There is nothing but bliss.

But we have to be willing to step out of the ordinary mind and our limited experiences of who we are. We have to be willing to take the giant step into the truth of love—not just in love-making and orgasm, but in all areas of our lives—over and over again until we incarnate that truth.

Love in its essence is about *union*. It is about merging and becoming one with the truth of who we are; one with the beloved; and—some might add—one with a still greater truth that dwells beyond all the illusions and limitations of the world of ordinary consciousness.

THE "THIRD WAY": HEIGHTENED CONSCIOUSNESS

What are love-making and orgasm *really* about? We can experience sexual pleasure on a physical level and consider it a thrill, using it to satisfy physical urges and emotional needs. Similarly, love-making and orgasm can be regarded as something mundane, a biological process that is part of our physical makeup. But there is a third way to see and understand these experiences: *as a means of raising our consciousness and moving to higher levels of energy.*

The heightened awareness and the energy of love experienced in this way can then be *held* and *carried* into other areas of one's life. The process is one of awareness and energy very naturally and freely flowing within and through oneself, eventually *expressing as oneself*. This energy can further flow beyond these experiences to touch and benefit others in ways seen and unseen.

A WORD OF CAUTION

We must never think of these matters as "high-minded," idealistic notions, philosophical abstractions, or wishful thinking. *They translate into experienced energies, ranging from harmonious, healthful sensations all the way to awakened joy.* Nor has anyone the right (or evidence) to deny this who has not attempted to be free from the destructiveness of mass-minded sensualism and the *minimal,* truly subhuman experience of sex and orgasm with limited understanding of their true nature and power.

For these reasons we take a hard look, in the Part that follows, at just what this destructive experience and its consequences consist in.

PART TWO

The False Uses of Love-Making

SEXUAL ENERGY PLAYS A VITAL ROLE in our mental, emotional, physical (and for many, spiritual) well-being. Having already looked at the joys that accompany genuine love-making, the misuse of love-making, on the other hand, poses numerous and complex problems throughout many levels of our being, including some that few of us know to exist.

The understanding and healthy use of sexual energy are not strictly a matter of morals or ethics, although moral and ethical considerations inevitably arise. *Nor are they a matter of judging oneself or others*. Instead, we want to understand some of the consequences and implications of the misuse of the body and sexual energy, including the psychological, the emotional, and the physical.

Misuse of the body and sexual energy is one of the principal maladies of our modern world, diminishing us as individuals, couples, families, and communities—and in some tragic cases even destroying us. It is a blight we bring upon ourselves unnecessarily through ignorance, misunderstanding, and what may be a fatal attraction to the seduction arts, especially those in the media and the entertainment industry.

This promotion of its misuse and the confusion of love with lust extend even into the most private recesses of our homes and minds. They go underestimated and unchallenged only at our very real risk. The harm, especially to the young, in fact is so pervasive and goes so deep emotionally, psychologically, and energetically that it can be seen as a species of individual and societal rape.

Once the seeds of lust have been sown in mind and heart, especially at an impressionable age when the mind is fresh and the heart innocent, the experience of true love in love-making is often foreclosed, with the individual trapped in a consciousness of loveless sex, perhaps never to know or experience what true love-making is.

What we require, then, is an *alternative* view—as seen through *love's* eyes—of the role of the body, sexual energy, and love-making in our lives. This view opens up for us a new panorama—one of health, beauty, love, and creativity.

In Part One we saw something of what occurs energetically in love-making. In Part Two we shall see in detail how misuse of the body and sexual energy works its harm. This information is meant to help us, especially the younger of us (1) to be more discriminating in our beliefs and attitudes concerning the place and use of sexual energy in our lives, and (2) *to make more informed choices about when, why, and with whom we experience this precious energy.*

Many have made mistakes in their choices of the use of sexual energy and have harmed themselves and their partners. We are *now* at a place where we can heal the wounds and undo the damage we may have already done to ourselves and others. We can do this in part with compassion and forgiveness, both for ourselves and others.

In this process, we can also ask ourselves the place that *merely sexual acts*—in contrast to love-making—may be having, or have had, in our lives. We can then see how we have used this sexual energy in the past, and the place and uses we might want this powerful and creative force to have in our lives now.

Do you love me because I'm beautiful,
or am I beautiful because you love me?

— OSCAR HAMMERSTEIN, II

3

energy blockages and imprints

T HE LIFE-FORCE AND SEXUAL ENERGIES, which flow from the same creative source within us, are the energies most involved in love-making. When they are joined with *love* energy—when they are expended and consummated in genuine *love*—these energies become *one* energy, an energy that is powerful, creative, and transformative, an energy that can work healing, renewal, and—taken to a high enough level— what some call "miracles."

ONSET OF IMPRINTS AND BLOCKAGES

When we use the life-force and sexual energies in an intimate relationship where love is not present, something very subversive happens to them—and to us. This is because it is the nature of these energies and the love energy to become *one* energy, to merge into *one powerful and creative force* that fills, transforms, and heals the lovers. This is at the core of what love-making is about.

For this to occur, the hearts of the lovers must be open and love must be present; and the energy centers corresponding to the life-force and sexual energies must also be open. However, when love is not present or the centers are closed and their energies not flowing, the movement and merging of these energies do not occur. As a result, the energy centers become blocked and the movement of energy becomes "stuck."

The reason this occurs is that *sexual intimacy when love is not present is a traumatic experience.* It creates what might be described as negative "imprints" in the energy centers and energy field—as though the experience of loveless sex were "impressed" upon us energetically and in other ways. These imprints block the movement and flow of energy in the energy centers and in the energy field. Because we are *energy-constituted* beings, the most immediate effects of sexual intimacy are therefore themselves energetic—i.e. in the realm of energies.

We may not sense loveless sexual acts as being traumatic or even negative on the conscious level. But at deeper levels within us, where we feel most intensely the need for love, we feel and carry these experiences as traumas. They are violations of our need for love, as well as of the power, integrity, and creativity of our sexual energy. And we carry a "history" of these traumas in the form of imprints and blockages in our energy centers and field. In turn, these energetic consequences affect us adversely on all levels, including the physical, emotional, and mental.

EFFECTS OF IMPRINTS & BLOCKAGES

These imprints and blockages can be felt energetically, and they can alter our attitudes and behaviors. For example, they can make us feel "closed off" sexually, causing us to lose a sense of aliveness in sexuality. Or they can trigger a compulsive urge for sex in an unconscious effort to unblock our sexual energies. The impulse may take the form of an assertive—even domineering—drive that seems to take on a life of its own.

If our sexual energies are not connected to love, they do, like cancer cells, take on a "life" of their own. Herein lies the problem. When our sexual urges and impulses are not connected to love, they invariably lead us *away* from love. In our attempts to satisfy them, we end up hurting ourselves and others.

So, whereas love-making is creative, contributive, and expansive, loveless sexual acts are destructive, subtractive, and *contractive*. They deplete our energetic force and vitality, they diminish the fullness of our humanity, and they contribute to a "darkened" sense within us. The misuse of sexual energies in any possible spiritual sense finds its complete undoing here.

The result could then become *habitual* failure to bring openness to intimate relations. The wounds of love run deep, and many people at some point defensively choose *not* to live with an open heart. *But we cannot be fully alive sexually or in other ways if our hearts are not open.* One of the most difficult challenges we all face in life is *not* to allow our suffering to close us off to love, but rather to let it take us *deeper* into love. Rarely, however, is this the response.

MERE SEX: A BETRAYAL OF LOVE

While merely sexual experiences may bring *physical* pleasure, they leave untouched our deeper longing for love, union, integration, and any (often unrecognized) inclination to experience the possible spiritual energies of love. What we experience in *mere* sex, then, is not love, but a *betrayal* of love, of our need and yearning for love. Whereas we experience the *fulfillment* of love in *love-making,* we experience a *betrayal* of love in *mere* sex.

Out of confusion or ignorance, we often turn to sex *in search of love* and the healing that love brings. However, in *mere* sex, our longing to become and embody love (and our need for healing) remains simply unfulfilled. Sexual acts *as such* are loveless experiences—at best, momentarily pleasurable *encounters*—but without love they cannot provide the identity, relationship, and healing we deeply desire.

Merely sexual acts, moreover, do not bring *freedom* or *bliss*. Nor do they bring us to heightened awareness or to a greater sense of who and what we are—and *can* be. On the contrary, loveless sexual acts limit our freedom and create still greater obstacles to our experience of bliss. They keep us at low levels of awareness. They dim our mental outlook and serve to demoralize us emotionally.

These are very high prices to have to pay for momentary pleasure.[*] At *some* level, consciously or unconsciously,

---

[*] One of the most prolific sources of self-deception—and of the perpetuation of habitually *mere* sex—is the illusion that this kind of activity can be the prelude to better-intentioned , "meaningful," sex-to-come, provided the relationship "works out." By degrees it becomes apparent that such relationships rarely ever work out, and the pseudo-search for love is resumed.

we *know* that in *mere* sex we have once again betrayed ourselves, and we can actually sense that we are carrying the effects of this betrayal in the form of imprints and blockages, which adversely affect our physical, mental, emotional, and even spiritual well-being.

USING EACH OTHER: MUTUAL BETRAYAL—AND INJURY

In loveless sexual acts we also experience a sense of *using* and *being used* in relation to another human being. Two people who do not love each other may *consent* to have sex. However, the mere fact of mutual consent does not alter the experience of the loveless act as traumatic and a betrayal of our deeper need for love. While one may believe that the experience has been harmless for oneself and one's partner, the energies tell a different tale. Both persons carry the effects energetically and in other ways, and may come to realize it only much later—if ever.

Sexual acts without love are a mutual betrayal of each partner's longing for love and need for healing at the deepest levels of being. Love *does* heal, and this is one reason we deeply long for love. Without it, we fail not only ourselves but also our partners. And of course when mutual consent is absent, the betrayal and trauma are even greater.

In sexual experiences without love present, betrayal becomes *injury:* both of ourselves and of our partner. The partner experiences the same trauma at the same level as we do and also carries blockages and imprints as a result of the experience.

NEGATIVE CONDITIONING

The imprints that form as a result can, moreover, act as a type of *negative conditioning* that has us responding in the same way over and over again to the same or similar experiences. For example, a person who has had many sexual experiences without love and carries deep imprints from them may have difficulty moving beyond these imprints should the opportunity for true love-making arise.

This is especially true when a person's initial sexual encounters are experiences of lust and are not connected to love. The experience of sexual energy then becomes associated with the nature of lust and not with the wonder and beauty of love. This is just one reason why the promotion and glorification of the misuse of the body and sexual energy are so damaging: we learn to link sexual energy with lust, not love. And for many, it may prove difficult to *un*link these associations and to dismantle the destructive learning.

ZOMBIES UNDER THE COVERS

Some people, if the imprinting and blockages set in deeply enough, begin to feel lifeless, emotionally armored, and zombie-like. The flow of life-force and sexual energies, which are the source of our sense of aliveness, is slowed down or stopped altogether.

The depletion and blockages of sexual and life-force energies may make us feel dead to these energies. In an attempt to feel alive again, some people engage in repeated acts of loveless sex as they try to unblock and reconnect to the energies. These problems can cause or contribute to *sexual addiction,* one of the most widespread but willfully ignored dependencies besetting us today.

Such behaviors only lead to more imprints and blocked energy—and further away from the love that one is really desiring. Dissociated from ourselves, we use—and allow ourselves to be used by—others and become *available playthings* to others. Or we are the predators ourselves. *Or we are both.*

Loveless sex is never harmless and hardly ever " innocent." *Sexual energies are powerful.* When used together with love, they are forces for our expansion as full humans. When used without love, they are forces that tend toward our dimming and shutting down—and for some, a spiritual dislocation.

NO MARRIAGE EXEMPTIONS

This is equally true for married and unmarried couples. Married couples who do not love each other and engage in sex are injuring themselves in the same way that unmarried couples do when they engage in loveless sex.

Without the presence of love in a marital relationship, sexual experiences create blockages and imprints here as well, and the couple will bear the trauma of the loveless experience. We are also looking at a strong reason why many troubled marriages fail in the presence of other factors that might have saved them: they are lacking in one of the most vital ways a couple has to connect with each other. These considerations alone dictate the wisdom of couples marrying *only* out of love.

INHIBITION AND REPRESSION OF SEXUAL ENERGIES

Blockages of life-force and sexual energies can also be caused by *inhibiting* or *repressing* them for psychological or emotional reasons. Some people deal with fear or pain that they may associate with the experience of these energies by blocking their flow. The (usually) unstated rationale is that if they can prevent themselves from feeling such energies, they are less likely to enter into an intimate relationship where they might be hurt. Some people simply fear the power of these energies, or for other reasons believe that they should not have a place in their lives.

Many are not even aware that they are inhibiting or repressing them: the action is often an unconscious one. But regardless of the reason, a person repressing or inhibiting these energies will not experience the fullness of life. *The activating energy for feeling this fullness is being denied.*

UNCONSCIOUS CONSEQUENCES

On a conscious level, most of us are not aware of the effects of our thoughts, emotions, and experiences on our energy centers and fields. Still, these centers and fields are *very reactive* to what we think and feel, as well as to the memories we carry from prior experiences.

Our emotional states and cognitive processes affect us in ways of which we are not usually aware; nevertheless, *everything* we feel and think impacts our energy centers

40

and field, often creating imprints and blockages that influence our behavior. Some of these manifest as patterns we continually act out; some are latent until triggered by a similar situation, then acted out by association.

Ultimately, the goal is to be a clear, clean energetic vessel with powerful, clean centers. For this reason, the energy centers and field routinely need to be cleared and cleaned out. Visualization, because it impinges on subconscious contents, is one way—but just one—of achieving this.

IMBALANCES, DISTURBANCES, AND DISEASE

Blockages and imprints not only cause a loss of vitality and create imbalances in our energy fields; they can cause psychological and emotional imbalances and disturbances as well. *They may even cause disease in the physical body.* The *energy* body, which holds the major energy centers, is the molder and supplier of energy to the physical body. When the energy centers are blocked and energy is not flowing, the physical body will be affected, and physical illness can result.

Physical illnesses often manifest in the energy field before they show up in the physical body. Blocked energy often exhibits as slow-moving or not moving at all. If these blockages are not cleared, over time they can result in physical illness in parts of the body corresponding to where in the energy body the blockage exists. The blockage or depletion of life-force and sexual energies, regardless of its cause, may be linked to such diseases as prostate and ovarian cancer.

We have been examining blockage at considerable length in order to prepare our awareness for the serious matter of *energy on the move between partners,* especially in its unwholesome aspect as negative, intrusive, and—if not recognized for what it is—injurious exchanges of energy.

4

exchanges of energies

W HEN SEXUAL INTIMACY IS EXPERIENCED between two people, there are *exchanges of energies* between them. It is the nature of sexual intimacy for these exchanges to occur. When we are sexually intimate, we are usually open energetically in very profound ways and on levels most of us do not even know exist.

The exchange of energies between partners is a kind of mixing or blending in which each partner is left carrying energy of the other. These exchanges of energies occur in love-making, sexual acts, and in intimate physical relations *even when intercourse does not occur.* (See UNSUSPECTED VENUES & ENCOUNTERS, p. 52.) Thus when two people are sexually intimate with each other, they take on each other's energies—and the *qualities* of those energies, both positive and negative.

THE NATURE OF THE EXCHANGES

Ideally, the energy exchanged is between two people who love each other deeply. The exchange is then positive: a sharing, with the beloved, of the beauty and grace of the love energy and the creativity and power of the life-force and sexual energies. If love is present and the energy centers are open, there can be a wonderful play of energies, creating still *more* love as well as an enlightened awareness *within* each partner and *between* them. However, when love is not present, the exchange of energies will be of a very different, unsatisfactory nature. These exchanges occur between the energy fields and energy centers of both partners. Thus, when we are sexually intimate with someone, we take on and carry their energy, and they take on and carry ours. Each carries the energetic "vibration" of the other's energy field and centers.

This vibration includes, to a greater or lesser degree, the other person's thoughts and emotions. These can be positive or negative, conscious or unconscious. For example, if we are angry or sad, the vibration of our anger or sadness can be transferred to a sexual partner along with the exchange of other energies, and the receiving partner will take on, usually unconsciously, the energy of anger or sadness.

ON THE RECEIVING END

The receiving partner will begin to feel these emotions usually after the sexual encounter has ended. The degree to which we are affected by the vibration of a partner's energy will be influenced by several factors, including the strength of our own energy field in relation to the partner's, and the vibrational *intensity* of the partner's thoughts and emotions.

Sometimes after having had loveless sex, some people feel they are carrying something "dirty" or something that is not really *theirs*. They may even feel the need to bathe—a kind of ritual cleansing—in an effort to rid themselves of these feelings.

On the other hand, when the experience is one of genuine love, such feelings normally are not experienced. Instead, each partner feels bathed in the energy of love in the afterglow of the love-making and wants to hold on to these feelings for as long as possible.

CARRYING THE PARTNER'S ENERGY, OR TIES THAT BIND

Sexual partners typically carry each other's energies for half a year or more. In fact, they will carry some of a partner's energies *indefinitely* unless they clear and release them. This means that *some energies of prior sexual partners are carried for the rest of one's life.*

Taking on and carrying a sexual partner's energy has many implications. We are, in effect, taking on something of our partners' *personality* and *past.* We do this willingly when we marry someone and assume the responsibilities of the in-depth interpersonal relationship that should come with marriage. On the other hand, if we do not know a sexual partner well, we may carry energy, possibly for the rest of our lives, that we wished we never had to deal with. And this without a clue to *how* or *why.*

These and other consequences discussed below point to the often unrecognized wisdom of having sexual relations with only one person, usually one's partner in marriage. (See MARRIAGE?, p. 94, for a discussion of the possible place of marriage in one's life.) We may rightly ask what worthwhile purpose is served by carrying other people's energies, whether for months or a lifetime.

The exchange of sexual energies between partners may cause them to enter into, or remain in, a long-term relationship that is not right for them. For example, after a so-called casual sexual encounter, each person walks away carrying energy of the other, creating a bond between them that may cause confusion about their real feelings toward each other. This is why so many "casual" sexual encounters often lead to long-term relationships that are not right for the partners—just one reason why it is important to be clear about what we feel for someone before we share ourselves sexually with that person. *When we are sexually intimate with someone, we are creating ties that bind.*

Carrying a partner's energy can be particularly problematic in the ending of a long-term relationship, especially if one of the partners wants to hold on to the other. As a result of the energies that each carries of the other, it may be difficult to completely sever the relationship, and the bonds may continue to be felt on an emotional or psychological—or even physical—level.

CONVEYANCE FROM PREVIOUS PARTNERS

In addition, the energies of *previous* sexual partners that one may still be carrying are passed on to *subsequent* partners, and vice-versa. This is particularly true of the most recent sexual partners. And exchanges of energy can be even more complicated when one or both partners are still sexually active with *other* partners. This type of situation will sooner or later pose a threat of *identity-loss* for those involved.

LOSS OF IDENTITY

Persons sexually active in this way pass their own energies and those from all *prior* and *current* partners on to any new partner. This is one reason why *persons who are sexually active with different partners can lose a sense of their own identity,* or else experience it as submerged beneath the identity of another. (See SUBMERGENCE, p. 48.) Our energy fields carry the unique qualities of who we are as individuals. *The more we carry the energies of others, the less we feel the energies that are uniquely ours.*

The sense of self is at high risk when one carries the energy vibrations of various partners—and their partners' partners in turn. The more energies of other people that one carries, the greater this risk is, as the cohesion and strength of one's energy field begins to diminish under the weight of other people's energies.

We also take on and carry aspects of the partner's *personality,* because the energies that are exchanged carry the vibration of the partner's emotions, thoughts, and prior experiences. In other words, *we begin to feel the vibration of the partner's energy as our own energy.* At the same time, of course, we are being weakened energetically by the blockages and imprints created in our energy fields as a result of engaging in sexual acts without love. Thus, *engaging in indiscriminate sex can cause severe injury ener-*

getically, as well as create serious problems emotionally and psychologically.

SUBMERGENCE

Persons who lose their sense of self may then find their identities increasingly submerged beneath another's. As they become weakened energetically and suffer an increasingly impaired sense of self, they are more apt to be overwhelmed by the force of another's personality, particularly one whose energy field may be stronger.

"CLOUD" EFFECT

The exchange of energy between partners engaging in sexual acts without love also creates what can be described as a "cloud" of dim or darkened energy around them. This acts as another stifling effect on the flow and vitality of each partner's energy; and because it is something they have in common, the "cloud" effect is yet another *bind* between them—a tie or bond, resulting from their mutual misuse of sexual energy, that they will carry until it is released.

Thus, *each time we have sexual relations with someone, we are creating enduring consequences for ourselves and the other person that we never imagined.* In these ways we continue to be linked with former sexual partners indefinitely *until the ties and bonds are released.* Section 5, RELEASING TIES & BONDS FROM PAST SEXUAL EXPERIENCES (p. 73), discusses the techniques and dynamics of this release.

"HOLES" IN THE ENERGY FIELD

Another effect of the exchange of energies in sexual acts when love is not present is what might roughly be described as "holes" or perforations in the partners' energy fields. Without the vital energy of love, the exchange of energies between partners can create gaps that weaken the energy field. In contrast, when love *is* present, the mixing or blending of energies *strengthens* each partner's energy field, because more love and the energy of love are created in the love-making.

While all of us are born with different amounts of energy, in most cases we are born with an *intact* and *vibrant* energy field, akin to a radiant garment designed to be worn throughout life. Energy "holes," or perforations, are therefore a tearing or ripping of this precious protective and life-supporting cover, the "moth-holes" of our radiant garment.

Holes in the energy field make it difficult to retain energy—or to restore it once it is depleted. So when we attempt to expand our energy fields (which is necessary for growth of every kind), we experience difficulty because the holes leave the energy field porous and less capable of holding energy. The "energy drains" commonly referred to by more and more people are frequently of just this nature and origin, though little suspected.

Once formed, the holes are not easy to "close"—the more so since most people do not even know that their energy fields are perforated. The consequences are similar to the situation of those who carry a malignancy without knowing it.

The fact is, *sex without love is itself a malignancy.*

SUSCEPTIBILITY AND FATIGUE

We have seen that the energy field fuels the physical body. An energy field weakened by holes may affect the physical body's capacity to fight off illness—*and fatigue as well.* And not only do holes in the energy field make us feel easily fatigued, so that we function at less than our full potential; they also limit the energy field's ability to buffer or filter out *external energies* that we may not (or should not) want to enter us. As a result, we can be highly susceptible to the thoughts, emotions, and other energies of the people and places around us.

At such times, we can be confused over which thoughts or emotions are coming from *within* ourselves and which are coming from *outside* of us. This is but another aspect of the identity crisis that is risked when energy exchanges occur in loveless sex—*and more so in promiscuous* sex, for reasons that by now should be fairly obvious.

SUBSTANCE ABUSE OF THE ENERGY FIELD

Holes in the energy field can also be caused by the use of *alcohol* and *drugs,* including many prescription drugs. So far from being surprising, this is one of the most noticeable evidences of overindulgence, dependence, and addiction in these areas. It is especially sad to see young people, most of whom have been blessed with vibrant energy fields, begin to exhibit this effect in their fields after beginning to have sex and use alcohol or drugs.

What may appear to be innocent experimentation or youthful folly injures young people, often seriously, in ways they do not suspect. And they can carry this damage for the rest of their lives. The large number of adults with holes in their energy fields is often the result of having engaged in indiscriminate sex or used drugs and alcohol—or both—in their youth.

It is equally sad to see young people with "perforations" of their energy fields as a result of the sustained use of *prescription* drugs to treat conditions such as depression or behaviors described as hyperactive or associated with attentional deficits. The damage done energetically may far outweigh any benefits resulting from the drugs. Healing should bring wholeness to us *energetically* (and in other ways) and not damage our capacity to be whole.

IMPLANTING NEGATIVE ENERGY IN THE OTHER

It can also happen in the exchange of energy that one of the partners places or "implants" negative energy in the other— consciously or unconsciously. We have to remember that *when we have sexual relations, our energy fields are usually wide open.* This constitutes potential vulnerability to negative, unhealthful inputs: at such times, it is easy for one partner to place his or her own negative energy into the other.

This can be done as an attempt (most often unconscious) to evacuate unwanted or intolerable thoughts or emotions; to control the partner; or to make the partner ill. Some people *do* become physically ill because their sexual partner is *regularly* implanting in them negative energy. *We are complex beings, and this complexity extends to the energies we carry and how they are transferred to others.*

For example, a man may find that he is having a greater-than-normal problem with anger. The problem subsides when he stops dating a woman with whom he has been sexually intimate. She could not tolerate her angry feelings, which she carried for most of her life, and put them energetically into him. It was when he began having sexual relations with her that he began to experience more anger; but he did not know why.

UNSUSPECTED VENUES AND ENCOUNTERS

Exchanges of sexual energies can occur between people in many different settings and under many different circumstances. Such unremarkable events as going to a supermarket or sitting in a meeting, for instance, can involve a mutual exchange of energy.

There are also *one-way movements of energy*. These commonly occur when one person experiences a strong sexual desire for another. Sexual energy is then conveyed from the person with this desire to the other person, who ends up carrying this projected sexual energy in his/her energy field if unable to resist it.

Society's concern with sexual harassment in the workplace has focused exclusively, as might be expected, on behavior of an *overt* kind: words and outward actions. Totally overlooked is the "subliminal" kind, which moves *covertly* in offices, corridors, and meeting-rooms. This may be mistaken for amorous feelings, resulting in faked business trips and lunch-hour liaisons.

If one is sufficiently sensitive to energy, one will actually *feel* it. Many do—without being aware of exactly *what* it is they feel. One, then, can and *should* learn to distinguish between feelings of love and feelings of lust. It is easy to become entangled in someone's sexual energy and feel that one has fallen in love.

For example, those subtle, seemingly inexplicable "moods" that are especially common in adolescents and young adults may be tied to the sexual energies they are carrying from friends and acquaintances. *Such moods are warning signals*—but they usually go unnoticed for what they are and unheeded for what they portend.

The types of energy movements and exchanges under discussion—which occur even if one or both parties are not conscious that they are occurring—are a misuse of sexual energy and a violation of an unwilling participant in it. Nevertheless, some people attract these types of movements and exchanges through the use of provocative clothing or suggestive grooming or behaviors, because they (consciously or unconsciously) want to attract or actually take another person's sexual energy.

In this latter case, they draw others' energies to themselves as a means of acquiring energy for themselves. We examine this seemingly straightforward but actually complex matter in the next section.

5

sexual energy in seduction

T HERE IS A REASON WHY some people choose to dress or groom themselves in ways that are *not* provocative. Advertently or inadvertently, they are responding to an awareness—inner or explicit—that their energy field is closely connected to the self-representation that clothing and grooming express. And if this is true of *appearance,* how much more so of *behavior*.

Certain ways of dressing, as well as certain uses of such things such as makeup, scents,* and jewelry, often elicit exchanges of sexual energy, even if unintentionally. We have to ask ourselves what purposes such exchanges might be serving and if we really want to risk them. These types of exchanges, then, can be still other ways in which the body and sexual energy are misused. The word *seduction,* in this context, is not misplaced and extends far beyond mere appearance.

If we go through the day projecting our sexual energy onto others or letting others take our energy, we divert that

---

* During the "sexual revolution" of the 1960s, much was made of the benefit of musk in men's colognes as a species of aphrodisiac. The most recent strategem is bottled pheromones, promising "No more lonely nights." Women's perfumes are perennially advertised as veritable potions, part of a female's arsenal of seduction.

vital force from the positive uses to which it should be directed. Likewise, if we go through the day attracting others' sexual energies or being carelessly open to receiving them, then we have to deal with the vibrations of those energies, which we end up carrying. *It is a senseless, confused (and confusing) way of being in the world and can lead to further confusion about who we really are and about the place of love in our lives.*

ENERGY VAMPIRISM

Seduction reflects such a senseless and confused way. The seducer extends his/her sexual energy out and into another person and, in a sense, "captures" that person (often referred to as a *conquest*). *The seductive energies literally come out of the seducer's energy field and into the other person.* They then draw, like a syringe, the energy of the other person, who has become a prey of the seducer. *There is a literal withdrawal of energy from the field of the person who is the target of the seduction.* This causes a loss of energy and pulls one out of one's own power. It also makes the seducer's work that much easier to consummate.

At the same time, the seducer's energy remains in the other person, *who then may confuse it with genuine feelings of love, or with attraction based on love.* However, unlike the energy of love that two people feel between them when they are in love, the sexual energy used in seduction is intended to create feelings of *physical attraction* and *sexual desire* that are all too easily mistaken for love.

But exactly the contrary is the case: such experiences have nothing to do with love or a *genuine* attraction or desire *based on love*. They are about the manipulation and taking of energy. Quite rightly this can be called a form of *energy vampirism.*

ENERGY VAMPIRISM ILLUSTRATED

A man walks into a store as a seductively dressed woman walks out. The man looks at her with desire and, without knowing it (consciously), opens himself energetically. The woman gives him a "friendly" smile and, at that moment, draws sexual energy from him (or out of his energy field). In this brief encounter between strangers, which took less than five seconds, he lost energy and she gained energy. Who won? Neither.

He was foolish to be lured into her trap and lose energy. *She* succeeded in taking his energy; and this will make her stronger in some ways. Yet she now has to deal with the vibration of *his* energy—whatever it may be—in *her* energy field. And as she becomes dependent on taking and using others' energies in this way, *she will increasingly lose her own sense of self.*

Some people become accustomed to these types of energy exchanges and may even feel that they are normal. The exchanges do not necessarily lead to sexual relations, and in most instances they do not. For some, they are a kind of sexual game-playing ("Who's Seducing Whom?") that they become very adept at.

But these energy exchanges are not without their consequences. They introduce energies that can act as toxins coursing through one's energy field, with disturbing effects energetically, emotionally, psychologically and even physically. This is particularly true of people who take in this type of energy *unsuspectingly*—all the while not wanting anything to do with it, or with the person from whom it comes.

SEDUCTION SCENARIO

Seductions of any type, with both males and females as the seducers and the seduced, are not about love. The seducer is motivated by the desire (more or less conscious) to pull another person into a relationship in which he or she can take energy and manipulate the other through sexual relations.*

A second, somewhat different example: Two people meet socially. One seductively projects his/her sexual energy into the other. The recipient carries it and feels the vibration of the other person. After their encounter, the seducer's energy remains with the other person, who then finds him-/herself having thoughts or feelings about the seducer, or at the very least with the seducer on his/her mind. *The seduced party may then mistake the experience as one of having been attracted to, or even fallen in love with, the other person.* Persons who are very needy emotionally may be particularly susceptible to this type of experience.

The seduction also can be *mutual*, with both people perpetrating this misuse of sexual energy. Many seek out

* The seducer may well be without a *conceptual* sense of taking energy, or of manipulating for this purpose; sexual relations may instead appear to be the sole objective. However, the desire is essentially one and the same, and the motivation to take energy cannot be much below the threshold of consciousness.

these types of encounters with like-minded people in order to satisfy a mutual desire for sex—and the mutual taking of energy. It probably requires even less than mere intuition to bring such a couple together

It might seem extraordinary that seduction could be *mutual* and at the same time devoid of the elements of genuine attraction or love—or even of *consciousness* of the seduction being practiced. Yet such is the unwholesome nature of seduction *per se* that people can be imagining or fantasizing relationships on a conscious level that are at total variance with the inner, dark reality, ultimately revealed in what occurs between them energetically.

Much the same can be said of *flirtation*. Flirtation is not always as innocent as it sometimes appears and often has the same dark, seamy underside as seduction. The consequences for participants' sexual energies should not be underestimated. Innocent as flirtation may seem to "common sense," little in the realm of sexuality is the exclusive preserve of common sense. Rather, much potential harm lurks in the shadowland of love's absence.

DESPERATION'S RUDE AWAKENING

Sadly, it is not unusual for people to feel they have fallen in love, only to learn later that they have been *seduced* and fallen under the spell of something other than love. *Our greatest longing is for love, and many of us are desperate for love and the freedom and bliss that love brings*—thus desperately searching for love, and easily deceived as to what love really is. *But desperation breeds self-deception.*

Instead of love, many people are lured—often pulled—into relationships and experiences that are dim, even dark. They are often confused, tricked, and seduced in the very depths of their mental-emotional being. They have been pulled into something that is a mere shadow of love. And their bodies are taken along for the ride.

The effects of this are frequently tragic and register vividly on the energy field of one who has been seduced and continually used sexually: the energy field is often filled with blockages, holes, and lusterless energies—as well as the energies of others. The person eventually becomes depleted and *subject to frequent illness* because of the low vitality and dimness of the energy carried.

ANTIDOTE TO SECUCTION

The antidote to the poison of seduction? *Greater sensitivity to energy and greater trust in our deepest intuitive feelings about ourselves and others*. Much silliness and naïveté have to be jettisoned. Both men and women need to be informed about the nature of these encounters. They also have to listen to what their hearts and bodies are telling them. It is important to know yourself well and not confuse others' thoughts and feelings with your own. Similarly, if you do not feel good about a sexual experience or partner, these feelings should not be ignored. *You are experiencing them for a reason.*

BUT WHAT ARE WE TAUGHT?

The behaviors we are describing are much the same for both men and women today. At a young age, boys and girls are being taught, through the media and the entertainment industry, the ways of seduction in the form of provocative dress and behavior—and sexually explicit behavior as well. More and more, popular culture is about seduction and the misuse of sexual energy. It has been taken to levels at which both men and women are equally adept.

Even young people's exposure to   sex "education" in schools raises the question whether it bears any relation to *love*. Do the schools mention this crucial factor? Or are they simply imparting the "safe" *mechanics* of sexuality: how to "do it"—and, in effect, get away with it. We must learn and keep in mind at all times: *our energy is our life-force*. When others take our energy, or we share it with others in harmful ways, we become compromised at the very core of our being.

The exchange of energy that takes place in seductive behaviors and in seduction itself is therefore emphatically *not* about love. It is about sexual desire that is not connected to love. *As such, it is to a great degree about control and manipulation* through the misuse of life-force and sexual energies. It seeks to "conquer"—or, in some cases, to *be conquered*.

Where there is genuine love, there is no desire to control, manipulate, conquer: two people meet and may have sexual feelings for each other, *but these feelings are inextricably tied to the energy of love.*   Being in love is *then* enriched by sexual intimacy and by the power and creativity of sexual energies.

RED LIGHTS, GREEN LIGHTS

Prohibitions against sex outside of marriage and against casual sexual encounters, which were found in most societies throughout the world until relatively recent times—and which are still to be found in many "traditional" cultures—were intended, in part, to protect people against seduction and other misuses of sexual energy.

The sexual "freedom" found in many societies today has been accompanied, unfortunately, by little or no understanding of sexual energies and the harm inherent in their misuse. Self-restraint need not be a blocking of sexual energy, but a way of redirecting this precious gift and celebrating it in other areas of our lives. As discussed below, sexual relations are not the only way for sexual energy to be alive and creative within us.

POSITIVE SHIELDING

Sexual feelings not anchored in love begin to diminish in direct proportion to the genuine presence of love. The reason for this is that *the energy of love is more powerful than any other energy, including sexual energy, and it has the power to transform negative sexual feelings*. We can learn to rid ourselves of *merely sexual* thoughts and desires as we come to live more from within, more from the mind of love.

At the same time, we have to learn to *shield* ourselves on an energetic level from unwanted sexual advances. This can be done in different ways. For example, you can reinforce your conscious and subconscious patterning in this vital area of thought and feeling by actually *visualizing* yourself encircled by a "shield" of light (notice how this would correspond to a protective "sheath" surrounding your energy field) and by *affirming* your intention that *no one's energy comes onto you, nor is your energy taken by anyone else.*

AFFIRMATIONS AND VISUALIZATIONS

As curiously simple as it sounds, this type of visualization and affirmation can be very effective. Our energy fields are highly responsive to our minds on both conscious and unconscious levels. This or something similar can be done before you go to work or into settings where you will possibly encounter the risk of negative energy exchanges. Visualizations and affirmations can be done any time, anywhere. Affirmations are generally more effective when spoken aloud.

Both techniques remind us that the role of *mind* and of *thought* must never be underestimated, since such energy exchanges are, ultimately, manifestations of thoughts and desires on conscious and unconscious levels. A strong and unwavering intention *not* to engage in such exchanges will act as a powerful source of protection.

SEXUAL DEFENSE

In the final analysis, we must be willing to defend our rights *in* and *to* love. This means, among other things, that *we have to defend ourselves energetically* and not allow ourselves to be pulled into, and suffocated by, sexual lures. Present all around us, they tend only to destroy.

It also means that we have to be awake to the forces that are shaping our attitudes, desires, and behaviors and those of the persons we love. The culture of seduction that has grown up around us has not come about by accident or chance. It has been *cultivated* in the media and is what we have sadly come to accept as normal in the advertising and entertainment industries, to name but two. It is reflected in the way we dress, the way we talk, and the way we conduct ourselves with others.

It is also reflected in our dreams and in the fantasies we encounter in the most private recesses of our inner worlds. Illicit exchanges of sexual energy are not "natural" to us. They are *learned* behaviors, a lowering of energies whose nature it is to lift us into a higher consciousness and into the experience of *genuine* love, which is our essence and what we most deeply desire. Our past experiences and what we have done to ourselves and others is not the way it *has* to be.

SEDUCTION OF THE INNOCENT

It is sad to see how entertainment and advertising induce young people to adopt seductive ways and become *themselves* objects of sexual desire. Children from an ever younger age are being taught to misuse their bodies and sexual ener-gies—*not even knowing they are doing so*. This is nothing less, really, than *the seduction of the innocent.*

We have tolerated this for too long, and now we are reaping what has been sown. The misuse of sexual energy is destructive personally, and collectively it acts as a cancer. In our confusion we have lost the sense of moral outrage at what we have allowed to be done to ourselves and our chil-dren. How a society relates to and uses the power and cre-ativity of the life-force and sexual energies determines whether it rises to greatness or "pancakes" under the weight of its own illness and delusions.

Having examined two forms of the misuse of sexual interaction—*energy exchanges* and *seduction*—we briefly visit a third: the outright taking (in many cases, a form of *robbing*) of sexual energy from sexual partners

6

taking energy
from sexual partners

TAKING OF ANOTHER PERSON'S ENERGY can occur not only in exchanges arising from seductive behaviors and encounters. It can also occur in the act of intercourse. When we are sexual with another person, we are usually open energetically. If a person is inclined to take energy from another at that time, it is easily done. *And taking can occur on the deepest levels during intercourse.*

As we have already noted, the person whose energy has been taken will often feel *depleted* after intercourse. This can occur even with married couples; and one or both partners may feel impelled to take energy because of a previous sense of being drained or depleted. This taking, as with most exchanges, usually occurs without one's awareness. The partners may not know on a conscious level that they are taking energy or having energy taken from them. *But they feel the effects.*

NO ENERGY SHORTAGE

Although we may not be aware of it consciously, at some level we all know that we need energy to survive and to thrive. Yet there is enough energy in and around us to make taking another's unnecessary. *Life abounds in energy. This world itself abounds in energy.* Although we have misused—and perhaps destroyed—much of it, there still remains an abundance of energy for all.

Thus, when we feel depleted or otherwise in need of energy, there are many ways—such as through meditation, affirmation, visualization, the arts, enjoyable reading, exercise, spending time in nature—and for some, prayer—through which we can recharge ourselves energetically. *We do not need to take from others.*

TAKERS AND TAKING

Yet some people are so confused or wounded that they feel (again, consciously or unconsciously) that they need to go through the world taking other people's energy. Often they are "takers" in general. Society abounds in this type. They take from others on many levels, and not only energies. "Share the wealth" is their tacit motto—*your* wealth. Takers of energy range from those who feel needy and lacking within themselves to those who are actually malicious in wanting to take from and destroy others.

It is not uncommon for one sexual partner to take energy from the other. And if one partner *continually* takes the energy of another, the person losing the energy can not only feel continually depleted or drained but can become *emotionally disturbed* or *physically ill*. It goes without saying that taking energy in this way has nothing to do with love. Conversely, the *exchange* of energy in genuine love-making has nothing to do with the *taking* of energy.

TAKING: AN ILLUSTRATION

Sometimes you can see the effects of this type of taking in couples who have been together for some time. One partner looks healthy and robust, the other partner continually appears tired and drained. While there may be different reasons for this, sometimes it is because one partner is taking from the other during or apart from intercourse, or both. In times of genuine need, we may need to draw on another's energy, and partners are likely candidates for this. But the *taking* of energy has no place as a regular occurrence in a relationship.

FLASHING AMBER

It is not uncommon for people to feel depleted energetically after having had sex. This can occur repeatedly with the same partner, including a spouse. When one experiences such a depletion of energy, it may be a sign that one's partner is taking one's energy. It can also be a sign that one is engaged in *sex* and not in an act of *love*.

Caution is needed here. One's fatigue should not be lightly attributed to others. "Frequently, when analyzed, the mental cause [of fatigue] will be discovered as a deep-seated resistance to conditions which the patient has found himself unable to change," writes Dr. Ernest Holmes. What might those conditions be? We have already seen some. But Dr.

69

Holmes also recognizes "general dissipation of the [energy] reserves." The truth behind this might well be *energy- taking*.

Love-making, in contrast, *fills* the partners with energy, although they may feel it in varying degrees, depending on their sensitivity to energy. If one regularly feels depleted after having had sex, it may be time to examine the relationship more closely and get to know one's partner better. It may also be important to know whether one has a tendency to be taken advantage of in these ways.

ENERGY-SENSITIVITY

We need to be *sensitive* to energy—our own and others'— and use this sensitivity to guide us in assessing situations, experiences, and *people*—especially in sexual relations. Unfortunately there are those, as we now know, who take energy because they feel they are lacking, as well as those who prey on others' energy with genuinely destructive intent. *It is not difficult to safeguard yourself against such people if you know that they exist and you are at the same time sensitive to your feelings energetically.* Regrettably, unwholesome exchanges and the taking of energies are commonplace, and we cannot afford to be naïve about them.

THE CHOICE IS YOUR OWN

The energy you carry is your life-force, and it will determine how effective you are in reaching your goals and experiencing fuller dimensions of self. The *positive* energy you carry is your "light." Without it, you will live in relative darkness. Therefore, it is important to be wise in the choice of what you do with your energy. This is especially true in regard to intimate relations.

There are times we may *choose* to give energy or share it with another. When people are ill, they need energy for healing. Sometimes, we are simply feeling "low" and need energy. A parent's giving a child energy is a beautiful act of love. If you choose to give another energy, *you do not have to give your own and deplete yourself.* You can draw energy from other sources.

. As we have seen, life itself is energy; it is literally all around us, especially in nature. We can even "create" energy through the power of the mind and the use of such expedients as affirmation and visualization. This is well known to many spiritual traditions in the form of prayer and spiritual practices. Focusing such resources on sexual intimacy can shed much light and dissipate as much darkness.

One very positive step that very few people can afford to dispense with in reordering energy relations is to release the ties and bonds carried over from past sexual experiences. This is discussed in the section that follows.

7

releasing ties and bonds from past sexual experiences

IT *IS* POSSIBLE TO RELEASE THE TIES AND BONDS with partners from past sexual experiences. If we do *not* release them, we continue to carry the energies of these people, and they continue to carry ours. We continue to be linked to them and they to us. There is no benefit in maintaining these links, and in most instances they are harmful to both parties.

CLANDESTINE PASSAGEWAYS

In some cases, unbroken bonds between former partners are the means by which they have access to—and influence—each other on multiple levels, including the psychic. We are therefore helping ourselves *and our former partners* if we break these ties and bonds. This can serve to free us *and them* by unblocking and letting go of these "hostage" energies, thereby increasing our capacity—*and theirs*—for emancipation and growth.

However, the process of releasing ties and bonds must occur on *several* levels, because the energies are carried on all these levels. While we may be aware of some of these levels, we are not always aware of others. *We are complex beings and exist on many different levels at the same time;* and the energies we carry on *all* the different levels affect us. Consequently, we have to use different approaches and techniques for releasing the energies on the different levels on which we carry them.

RELEASING ALL FORMER PARTNERS

One may feel the need to release the energy of a particular past partner or partners. *However, it is best to release the energies from all past partners.* The process then is uncompromisingly one in which the ties and bonds with *all* prior sexual partners are broken. These include all partners with whom we have ever had intimate sexual relations—and not just intercourse.

A person may not remember all past partners. Or, for those who believe in past lives and the influence of relationships from past lives on current lifetimes, logic would require that partners from those other lifetimes be released as well. But how in such a case would we know *whom* to release?

In all events, we can *intend* to release any ties and bonds we may carry from such experiences as we go through the process of releasing. *Intention is of the essence.* Mind, including belief, is key to the process, and it is what we are primarily dealing with here.

THE PROCESS OF RELEASE

There is no one-only way to go about this process of release. What works for one person may not be suited to another. The best approach is to use the ways that most serve to open one up to one's inner truth and to create a clear and strong intent.

In the process, try to recall each sexual partner and attempt to determine the types of ties or bonds that you may have with him or her. These can include unresolved emotions, such as anger or hurt, or ties that come from having brought children into the world together. On an emotional and psychological level, *ties and bonds must be recognized and released* in order to be completely free of a past sexual relationship.

The releasing of these ties and bonds can be done in different ways. Avowal, promise, declaration, visualization, prayer, meditation, ceremony, and ritual (however one understands these processes) can be used alone or together for this purpose.

Note that ties and bonds that we do *not* recognize also may exist—*especially on deeper levels*. The same methods, together with the genuine *intent* that all ties and bonds be released, can be effective for these levels as well. Where religious beliefs are held, the invocation of revered beings can facilitate the process.

Some Native American wedding ceremonies include a ritual for just such a release. Prior to the wedding ceremony, each partner spends time in quiet and prayer and goes through the process of the release of energies from a former partner or partners and the asking of mutual forgiveness. A knot is tied in a cord for each of the former partners. During the wedding ceremony the cord is thrown into a fire and burned, marking the release of all former partners. Ancestral spirits are invoked to assist in this process.

RECLAIMING OURSELVES

Once we create within ourselves the necessary intent and then embark upon the process, it is not an option for the former partner *not* to release our energy. As part of the process, it is important that we make a mental *demand*, unequivocal in intent, that the energies we carry from former partners be released.

We must also be unequivocal in our intent that *our* energies, which *they* may be carrying, be "returned" to us. This is really nothing more or less than *reclaiming ourselves,* while at the same time restoring to former partners what is rightfully theirs. There is no magic or mystery involved. Our integrity and wholeness are ours by *right,* and they need not be lost to us—certainly not irretrievably—if we choose to safeguard and carry them with us throughout our lives.

TOUCH OF FORGIVENESS

It is also important that in our heart we ask each former partner to forgive us—and affirm that *we forgive the partner:* for the use of sexual energy without love is damaging to *both* partners; and almost invariably, these experiences involve using—and being used by—another. *It is also important to forgive oneself.* There are few among us who have not made mistakes in this area.

Former partners will normally not know we are releasing them and asking that they release us. But the release, as well as the forgiveness, *will* be effected on the only levels it needs to be; and we may reasonably expect that former partners will benefit from the release even though they may not be aware of it on a conscious level. Both the release and the forgiveness are gifts we give to ourselves and to others.

"Throughout eternity, I forgive you ... you forgive me"
— BLAKE

FACING PAST, FACING PAIN

The burden of past sexual experiences that were not of love may be heavy, and facing them may be painful. The purpose of all such releasing, however, is not to fall into judgment— of oneself or others—but to let go that which is not love in order to become that which *is* love: to become and be what we *can* be. Remorse is a normal reaction to the realization that one has injured oneself and others through a lack of love. But remorse can give way to joy as one faces one's errors and, through releasing them, becomes freer and more open to love.

The matter of becoming freer and more open, and the alternative to misusing sexual energy, is part of the *responsible* use of sexual energy, the subject of Part Three.

PART THREE

The Responsible Use of Sexual Energy

P URITY IN THOUGHT AND ACTION has traditionally been considered the alternative to the misuse of sexual energy and is continually referred to as *chastity*. Today the words *purity* and *chastity* in this context have come to be associated by many with moral theology, or else with a doctrinaire and antiquated, if not impossible, standard of morality—one increasingly repudiated, defied, and in any case neglected.

Whether or not termed *chastity,* the *responsible* use of the body and sexual energy has a rightful, salutary place in our lives. *Sexual relations without love do not satisfy our deepest desires*; they do not bring us love or healing. We are confused and acting out of ignorance or (self-)deception if we think they do. Nor do they do lead to a more *passionate* life—but rather to a loss of the passion *for* life.

As we deplete ourselves energetically, we no longer have the energy to fuel our passion and make of our lives something extraordinary. The misuse of sexual energy leads over time to boredom and a sense of *numbness* to the wonder and beauty of life. Life takes on a dullness as we dissipate our energies and no longer have the power to become who we really can be. Unfortunately, the area of our lives that can bring us great joy has become for many a source of great suffering.

It is not our purpose here to become involved in *moral* issues or teachings as such, but rather to approach the entire subject, as we have been doing, from the vantage point of *experience*—to see what hurts and what does not; what helps and what does not; what works and what does not; *what brings us closer to the truth of who we are—and what takes us further from that truth.*

Where there is great love, there are
always miracles.

— WILLA CATHER

8

sexual integrity

I NTERESTINGLY, *CHASTITY* HAS SEVERAL DEFINITIONS recognized by the dictionary:

- abstention from unlawful intercourse
- sexual purity
- purity in conduct and intention
- personal integrity

From these it can be seen that where *all* parties and philosophies can converge is at a point definable as sexual *integrity*. This is the term we shall adopt. By it we shall intend nothing that is not directly experiential. By it we shall mean what manifestly leaves us feeling—and being—fuller and more connected to the truth of who we really are.

Sexual integrity is inextricably linked to the effects of our use of sexual energy. Any "ethics" of sexual behavior is therefore *also* inextricably linked to the energetic effects of sexual intimacy—which in turn are directly tied to the presence or absence of love.

SEXUAL ENERGY: THE CREATIVE LIFE-FORCE

What moves us closer to becoming fulfilled in love is to begin the experience of being *filled* with love. At *some* level within us, we all know love. *It is our true nature.* Our task—what we must do in order to make our lives truly extraordinary—is to *expand* the love we already know in some degree.

Sexual energy is an important element in this task. The fact is, *we use this energy in everything we do and everything we are.* Its use is not limited to sex or to love-making: *it is the creative life-force,* ranging from the physical to the psychobiogical to the mental/emotional—and beyond. As such, this energy is in abundant evidence, even in children and infants. Our task is to protect it, nurture it, and let it grow.

LOVE - MAKING'S VARIETY

Love-making is a principal use of the sexual energy. It brings sexual energy to life and connects it to the feelings of the lovers in a unique way. But love-making itself can occur in many ways: meditation; spiritual practices; acts of selfless giving; the beauty of nature; laughter and joy—all of them involving *sexual* energy.

It is precisely here that so much thinking on this subject is ignorant, impoverished, or simply shabby. For the masses, whose consciousness is formed largely by popular culture, the use of sexual energy = copulation, intercourse. You either *do it* or you don't *do it* (subtext of the breezy

84

aphorism *"Just do it!"*). No instruction that they have ever had—by parents, at school, wherever—has prepared them for the idea that *sexual energy* is their overarching life-force, with love-making its supreme (but not exclusive) human expression, finding outlet in a wealth of ways.

Sexual energy is, then, an extraordinarily powerful force. It should be used only in ways that will bring it more fully to life in us, expand our energy fields and ourselves with them. If we choose *not* to engage in sex, the energy is still alive and active in us, firing our passion for love and life in countless other ways. Thus a *celibate* life—or celibate periods in our life—does not mean that we are any less connected to sexual energy.

CELIBACY: ONE FORM OF SEXUAL INTEGRITY

On the contrary, celibacy simply means that we opt to experience sexual energy *outside* the realms of physical love-making, or sex. If we work with this energy in meditation or visualization, for example, or stay connected to it in other ways, it will still be serving its purpose of opening us to our essential love and bringing us closer to any possible fuller expression of ourselves, including the spiritual.

Celibacy, in which the life-force and sexual energies are connected to the mental and emotional feeling-nature (and often directed spiritually), may be preferable to the married life for some people who for different reasons may be incapable of—or choose not to be in—an intimate love relationship during part or all of their lives. For example, a young adult may not yet have met a partner with whom he/she would want to make the type of commitment that love-making calls for. Or a widowed person may choose not to enter into another intimate relationship.

As we have already seen, experience of our fullness requires the opening and expansion of the energy centers and field in order to rise to and maintain an enlightened level of awareness. The life-force and sexual energies, which are necessary to this end, can be vibrant, and we can be "connected" to them whether we are sexually active or celibate.

CELIBACY: AN INFORMED CHOICE?

This book neither teaches nor counsels celibacy. People choose celibacy for many reasons. Some choose it out of fear of intimacy or fear of the power of sexual energy. Others understand the nature of this energy and even attempt to use it for spiritual attainment. Thus, for many Eastern monks, celibacy is a choice to experience sexual energy entirely apart from love-making with another. Their goal is to use sexual energy to bring them to a consciousness where they are in an intimate love relationship with the divine.

Many people have construed Jesus' life and message in the gospels as favoring celibacy. Jesus' message was and is *love*. Sexual energy, when linked to love, opens us still more to love. In fact, we cannot experience the fullness of love without sexual energy. As we have seen, it is the nature of love and the sexual energies to join and become one, making for a powerful and creative fusion. What we know of

Jesus and the force of his personality suggests that his sexual energy was fully alive in him.

In any scheme of things spiritual, the divine would have to work through our energy centers and field and not apart from them. This may be why persons reputed to have achieved high levels of spiritual attainment have exhibited energy fields that seem large and vibrant. On that view, the energy field would be a "container" for Spirit, and the more one expanded one's energy field, the more one could be filled with, or at least experience, Spirit. Conversely, the more Spirit dwelt within one, the greater would be one's energy field.

Some, then, may choose celibacy because they believe it is a superior way for purposes of spiritual attainment. Scripture and other sacred texts in many religious traditions are often cited as authority for the rule of celibacy. However, many celibates do not know what to do with their sexual energy. Some block or repress it out of a misunderstanding of its nature and purpose. But the task, whether one is celibate or not, is to *honor this extraordinary energy and ensure that it is alive within one*.

ONE ENERGY, ONE LIFE, ONE LOVE

What is supremely important is that we have access to *all* of who we are, and that our energies be connected to love so that we *become* love. The flow and expansion of energies are not dependent on love-making. Neither are they absent from it. Thus, people who are celibate permanently or only at certain times of their lives can also experience the openness and flow of these energies. *Ideally, the flow of these energies throughout the energy field is occurring continuously in every person, whatever his or her status, whatever his or her age.*

Perhaps the sexually "ethical" note to be struck here is that *whatever* promotes this flow is *sexual integrity,* because it is congruous with our energy fields and with ourselves as complex energy systems. Thus our attitudes and behaviors play a critical part in how we manage ourselves in this way. They would therefore not necessarily be of a theoretical, theological—or even moral—nature, although these considerations certainly have a place in shaping our sensibilities and ethics about the use of sexual energy.

Our attitudes and behaviors will instead be based on *experience;* there will be no room for naïveté and self-deception. Self-estrangement, lethargy, insensitivity, masochistic zombie-ism, and energy vampirism could then cease as ghastly substitutes for a sexual lifestyle. Emotional numbness and meaninglessness could vacate our feelings. Negative emotions, moodiness, anger, and depression would not find so ready a roost within us. Blockages, holes, and negative imprints would no longer be the norm and would instead shrivel to their native nothingness.

NECESSITY OF CHOOSING

All these changes can occur if people are informed and use their energies wisely. However, we need to keep in mind that in the past, great civilizations, such as the Aztecs, Mayans, and Egyptians, *knew* about these energies and misused them. Today, in many parts of the world people who know better misuse them quite deliberately. Understanding these energies allows us to make more informed choices, *but we still have to choose*. So all the changes mentioned *could* happen; but still, people have to *choose*.

AN END TO SELF-PROGRAMMED ABUSE

A greater understanding of sexual energy, combined with teaching about it in families, schools, churches, and its incorporation into the healing arts on all levels, could radically alter our lives and communities. We would not find ourselves implicated in a world of sexual abuse, rapes, unwanted pregnancies, disease, abortions, repressions, sadism, masochism, etc.

We would find pain *painful,* not pleasurable. We would have no gut-wrenching decisions to make that sacrifice one kind of good for a *suppositional* other kind, one person's happiness for another's. We would avoid the necessity for energy-detoxification and other species of withdrawal. We would not have to carry through our lives the personal and often painful legacies of choices based largely on ignorance, as well as on the pervasive (and subversive) influence of popular culture.

We could wean ourselves off the pathetically substance-less, impoverished content of so much that calls itself "entertainment." We would be impatient with, and repelled by, the trivialization and poisoning of our feeling-nature at the hands of demeaning sensationalism. We could retrieve a better sense of our own dignity from the clutches of the media maestros who would pervert it for the sake of ratings and revenues.

We could also be forever immune to the suggestion that sexual energy is "dirty"; that sexual desire is somehow "bad." Fear and guilt connected to these areas could begin to depart our lives. We could *truly* know what it is to live with passion, one that leads to harmonious sexuality, higher states of awareness, and enlightened living. Or we could know, if we preferred, how to live with sexual energies engaged *outside* the realm of the physical. The unsatisfactory does not have to be "the way it is" for ourselves, our children, or our children's children. *But the choice is ours.*

9

being what we *can* be

IT IS TIME FOR US TO RETHINK our beliefs, attitudes, and behaviors about the use we make of our sexual energies. *How* and *with whom* we use these energies are among the most important decisions we shall ever make in life. The consequences are immediate for the entire gamut of life lived, from the raw physical to the subtler mental and emotional levels we inhabit, to whatever higher-mindedness we may aspire toward, whether ethical, philosophical, or spiritual—or all of these, seeing that they are components to be found in us all.

EXCHANGES OF ENERGY WITHIN A BOND OF MUTUAL LOVE

In contrast to so much of what we have seen in Parts One and Two, when two people are committed to each other in a mature bond of love, they *willingly* take on and carry each other's energy. Some of the energy they take on from each other may be negative: most of us have flaws and imperfections that we carry energetically, as well as on other levels. But this is part of the commitment we make in love that strives to be unconditional. *We willingly accept both the positive and negative of the other person,* and this includes what they are carrying energetically.

THE FAIR EXCHANGE: HEALING

When love is present, much of the energy that is formed and exchanged during love-making is creative and healing. The love-making and the ensuing exchange of energies actually have the power to *clear away* negative and dark energies that the lovers may be carrying. This is one of the great, but often unrecognized, benefits of love-making. *It can actually be a source of healing.*

This includes *physical* healing. Many illnesses are caused by problems in the energy centers and by depletion—or by imbalances in the energy field—which are discussed in the following sections. The movement and fusion of energies in love-making can actually keep the energy centers open and their energies flowing and the energy field full and vibrant with energy, *preventing* or *removing* the conditions in the energy field that could manifest in the physical body as disease.

THE FAIR EXCHANGE: TRANSFORMATION AND COMMITMENT

Love-making can also be a source of *transformation.* When our thoughts and feelings are unencumbered by negative and dark energies, we have a better chance of becoming our best. That is, we can move into the highest frequency of energy, which is love.

This is what we can aspire to in love-making—but only within a relationship where there is a genuine and deep bond of love *and* commitment between the partners. This is the context that love-making requires. To open ourselves to another and to love deeply requires trust—and trust calls for *commitment*. Let us, for a moment, examine commitment.

"FOR BETTER OR FOR WORSE"

When we fully commit to another in love,we willingly accept both the positive and negative of the other person, *and this includes what they are carrying energetically*—because what we carry energetically is a part of who we are that we bring to the relationship. *But we do so only with a positive adjustment in view*. We strive together, in love and mutual support, to confront and let go of all that is not love. Here we see another level of meaning in the old words "for better or for worse" used in the traditional marriage vow.

But why would we accept and strive, even in these positive ways? Because we are now moving *in love,* which, while certainly not a mortgaging of self to abuse or sacrifice, nonetheless constitutes a willingness to share from our own store of good. *Energetic give-and-take* lies at the heart of bonding and makes of two persons the desired *one* that robs neither of anything but instead confers only good, each upon the other. And it is only within a context of love that this energetic give-and-take can heal and bring the lovers to a oneness.

WHAT *IS* THIS COMMITMENT?

Commitment in the exchange of sexual energy lies precisely within the *exchange* itself. Love does not, cannot, horde. In love, energy is never arrested, thwarted, stifled. In the healthy person open to the exchange of energies in love, there is no "armoring" or "steeling" of the emotions, the nerves, or the muscles against a prospective misuse, abuse, or other depreciation of energies, feelings, or body.

Commitment here means being what the French call *engagé*—the very opposite of being alienated, distant, aloof, suspicious. It is rather *total nakedness*—in more than just body—in the presence of the one chosen to receive and give sexual energy, its roots in the very depths of our energy centers and total energy field.

Commitment, then, is much, much more than anything that boils down to words or statements. It is a state of being, wholly *SELF*-ish in the best sense of the word. And it is also the willingness to give oneself wholly to the other, where two can become one. For many, it is in love-making that this sense of oneness is first experienced.

MARRIAGE?

Commitment in this context naturally suggests marriage. And although marriage is not a requisite for the highest expression of sexual energies, it is a "summit" of sorts in the realm of love-making—but again, not necessarily for all the "traditional" reasons.

In its own highest expression, *marriage is a special relationship in which two persons jointly and reciprocally commit to a life of love.* This is the primary reason two persons should marry. If they truly strive to love each other and live that love with all their hearts, minds, and bodies, the relationship will carry the potential to transform them at their deepest levels.

In this sense, marriage provides the "container" for the feelings that begin to come alive in us at the initial stirring of romantic love. As the lovers open more to each other and to love, they can transcend the limitations of the *ordinary* mind and move into a consciousness of love found in the *awakened* mind, and closer to a oneness with each other. It is when we move into this "mind of love," which opens to us in love-making and orgasm, that the experience of oneness becomes possible.

This is what we most deeply desire in romantic love, and it is a formidable achievement, one that cannot be gained through a relationship where a genuine bond of love and lasting commitment are not present. And we would be naive to believe that love goes unchallenged by powerful forces within and outside ourselves. Without an abiding commitment to each other and to love, which in most cases is found only in marriage,* lovers run a great risk of losing their way and of having their love for each other run aground.

---

* Let us reserve judgment just how and where this proves—as indeed it does—to be *characteristically* true and instead acknowledge the power of love to assert itself in even the unlikeliest of relationships, recalling, too, that one of the requirements of love is that we also "love one another."

Marriage, then, is meant to *"seal"* the love between the lovers. It is a means of sealing a union between two people striving together to achieve something truly extraordinary in their lives and relationship. And that sealing affords an indispensable element of defense against those forces inimical to love that the lovers must not ignore or underestimate if their love is to survive and grow.

Naturally, marriage cannot create that love—although its power, once engaged and committed to, could reverse many an unwholesome background or bad beginning. As a *seal,* though devoid of magical powers, marriage can confer a special protection on the love and the relationship. Among other things. it can bring in light and help to shut out the dimness of misbegotten energies. For the "seal" is in the minds and the hearts of the lovers.

Each partner in a marriage in which love is present can be the *minister* of love to the other. In this ministry our deepest wounds can be healed. Partly, this takes place in the energetic "give-and-take": the willingness to take on each other's energy in the framework of a *commitment* in which the lovers, as individuals and as a couple, strive to be all they *can* be. They thus become of *much* benefit and blessing to and for each other

MARRIAGE THE "DIALYZER"

The healing that can come through marriage is a process somewhat comparable to dialysis, in which poisons or impurities are separated out from the healthy solution. Here, the impurities, which take the form of thoughts, emotions, and the effects of past choices—all of which we carry as energy—are those parts of ourselves that are *not* of love and that act to obscure the love that is our essence.

In romantic love, each partner goes through a process of purification in what can be a wholly wordless, nonconceptual, interactive way, love being the sole "filter." *This process will be facilitated if each partner is anchored in some form of conscious striving for greater openness and self-awareness,* such as meditation, healthy introspection, analysis, counseling, prayer, or insightful spiritual practices.

A process of purification is really unavoidable in love. As the love between the lovers comes alive, it is as if the light of their love illuminates and draws out of them their inner darkness—those parts of their personalities that are not of love. The emergence of these impurities, while difficult and at times painful to deal with, offers one the opportunity, often otherwise avoided, to face and deal with those parts of oneself that prevent one from knowing and becoming the fullness of love that one can be.

Marriage is therefore a *process*—one in which we can come to know ourselves and have the opportunity to filter out the poisons we carry, which are certainly not of love. Likewise, we can help our partner do the same. Most of us carry energies—"impurities"—that can undermine the love that was the basis for the marriage. Viewed another way, then, this process is the "alchemy" of love, which can be experienced in a special way in marriage.

MARRIAGE THE CHALLENGER

Marriage, then, presents us with a challenge it quite rightly poses: to love and to be loved *in commitment and reciprocity*. In our human condition, although love is what we most deeply desire, it is not always simple or easy to love and be loved. Any "simplicity" or "ease" has to be worked out on many levels, all of them as complex as we ourselves are.

At our deepest level, we long to be whole *in relation to another.* We long to know and be known, to love and be loved, *by another*. Ultimately, then, most of us long to find that other, that partner, with whom we can experience pure love and become one. And we are, in a basic way, unfulfilled until we do.

This longing to join and become one with another is a defining characteristic of romantic love. To this some will add that the desire to become one with the beloved in romantic love is an expression of the soul's greatest longing: to become one with the divine.

SEEKING AND FINDING

But *who* is this other we passionately desire to join with, and how do we even know there *is* such a person with whom this union is possible? Moreover, if there *is* such a one, how do we find him/her? And if we feel we may have found this person, how do we know for sure that our desire is not misguided and that we are not mistaken about the proper place he/she occupies in our lives?

These questions, not simple in the asking or the answering, relate to the complexity of who we are and who the other person is—and to the complexity of the universe in which we live. Although they are difficult, they are not without answers. If we look deeply within ourselves, when we still our minds—as, say, in meditation—and listen to what we have to say to ourselves in naked candor, we can receive answers to these and other seemingly unanswerable questions. Simplistic—even naïve—as this may sound, it is a truth grounded in various and repeated findings of the psychological sciences themselves.

Our subconscious makeup carries a deeper knowing than our conscious does of who we are, what we are searching for, and what we truly need in a relationship and marriage. When we listen to this "inner wisdom" (some call it *intuition*) and pay attention to the answers that emerge, they offer guidance along the often confusing and sometimes perilous pathways of human relationship and love. If we come to know the truth of who we are in our deeper recesses, we can begin to shed some light on these vexed questions.

AND ON THAT DEEPER LEVEL …

What we have to give, then—what we bring to union—will never be more or better than what we have arrived at deep within ourselves, in that realm where subconscious patterning takes shape and then creates our circumstances after its own image. Attention to this will require real "homework," for, as Dr. Raymond Charles Barker was fond of asserting, *Happiness is an inside job.* However, there is no more important, more constructive job available than this one on *ourselves*. It is a process that takes us from the ordinary mind, with its endless delusions, to the mind of love, with its endless possibilities.

We begin, then, by consciously letting go of the delusions that keep us distracted from our truth and engaged in idle diversions and senseless activities—especially any that are implicit of *mere* sexuality. We also consciously reject the attitude that deludes so many (especially via the media) in which sex is essentially *juvenilized* by the assumption of "naughty," "bad," "daring" behavior, promoting teen-like defiance and rebellion, with a derogatory approach to sex as either *dirty* or else *"cool"* and *"far-out"*.

If we work to purge ourselves of negative conditioning and the subconscious patterning of what is not love, we *can* hold on to the heightened awareness and enlightened vistas that we encounter if only for short periods in love-making and orgasm. *These periods will gradually lengthen, and the intervals between them shorten,* as we abstain from their contraries in shabby and destructive experience—and as the truth we experience in love-making and orgasm extends into other areas of ourselves, our relationships, and our lives.

BEYOND LOVE-MAKING AND ORGASM

In orgasm—the moment central to the flow and exchange of sexual energies in the context of love—and in love-making in general, we confront two simultaneous journeys: *giving* to another all that we are, and *being* for ourselves all that we yet can be. The two are ultimately one.

At the same time, this experience does not belong to us alone. It connects us to the broader world in new ways as we bring the experience of more wholesome living to others and to our activities in the world. We are not meant to live love in isolation. As we connect more to love, and see more through the eyes of love, we can experience our oneness with others and with all of life.

GIVING WHAT WE ARE

We are journeypersons to our identity in love. It is not that there is nothing *better* to be; it is that there is nothing *else* to be. Love is the source and ultimacy of all energy, of all being.

This questing is also what ensures that, in relationship with another—on the deepest energetic level, which we experience in love-making—we are honoring all that the other is, contributing to all that the other can be. That is, by being true to our journeyperson-self in love, we cannot be false, manipulative, callous, selfish—*or foolish.* Foolishness is, in fact, the single most elusive factor in the tragedy of those *outside* of true love. There are few villains but, alas, many *fools*.

Instead, then, of being villains or fools, we are offering the best of ourselves for appropriation in love and partnership with another, whose fulfillment in this will find him/her atop the same summit of being that we are striving to attain.

101

BEING WHAT WE *CAN* BE

Finally, *we can be love itself*. This is no empty claim. It may seem wishful only because of our habituation to the less. But with heart and mind open, we have immediate access to who we are at the highest frequency of energy, which is pure love. There we can experience a bliss that owes nothing to form, thought, or ego. *Not that it will deny, repudiate, or invalidate these things.* Strikingly, they find their fulfillment in precisely that which *transcends* them.

We are, then, using the experience of love-making—an *interaction*—to make this discovery about *ourselves*—to claim this *identity*. But in the interaction, we are not *using* the one we love. In such an undertaking, this too is the lover's experience: *the discovery of being love itself.*

The result is not *twoness* but *oneness:* one life, one love, one identity. If there is any "higher consciousness," this life in love alone points the way.

Say, rather, it *is* the way *itself*.

And the day came when the risk to remain tight
in a bud was more painful than the risk it took to
blossom.

— ANAIS NIN

about the authors

MICHELLE RIOS RICE HENNELLY is a healer. She received a BA from the College of Santa Fe and a MSW from New Mexico Highlands University.

ROBERT KEVIN HENNELLY is a former attorney and currently a psychotherapist. He received a BA from the University of Notre Dame, a law degree and MS in Foreign Service from Georgetown University, and graduate degrees in counseling and clinical psychology from Pacifica Graduate Institute and the Fielding Institute.

Thank You!

for selecting this book from DeVorss Publications. If you would like to receive a complete catalog of our specialized selection of current and classic Metaphysical, Spiritual, Inspirational, Self-Help, and New Thought books, please visit our website or give us a call and ask for your free copy.

DeVorss Publications
devorss.com • 800-843-5743